GRANDMA MATTIE GETS HER MAN

SARAH TUCK

Copyright © 2016 by Sarah Tuck

This is a work of fiction. Names, characters, places, and incidents either are the product of the author's imagination or are used fictitiously. Any resemblance to actual persons, living or dead, events, or locales is entirely coincidental.

All rights reserved. No part of this book may be reproduced or used in any manner without written permission of the copyright owner except for the use of quotations in a book review.

Sarah Tuck Books for adults/18-years and older

Readers/Authorship: Play

Manufactured in United States of America

First Edition

Library of Congress in Publication Data

ISBN 978-0-578-43433-9-(book)

ISBN 978-0-578-43647-0 (e-book)

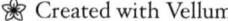 Created with Vellum

CHAPTER ONE

Grandma Mattie Gets A Man

Grandma Mattie hardly went anywhere; she is always in the house watching her favorite movie while sitting in her living room; she would watch her favorite television show Gun Smoke at the same time every day.

Her granddaughter Tina has arrived, and there she sits in her rocking chair watching her favorite show and making small talk with herself.

"Don't you ever get tired of sitting at home all alone with nothing to do?" Tina said with a smile on her face. Tina was in her late twenties, with a cute short hairstyle and big loop earrings. Her medium bronze lipstick made her face glow with the accent make up that she wore.

Grandma Mattie turned and looked at her as if she was crazy with her remote in her hand.

"Who says I'm alone?" Grandma Mattie asked. "Why, I've got Jesus that takes care of me, and not to mention I go out at least once a month to eat and spend time with the ladies from the church."

Tina was looking at a paper, then she folded it up and laid it on the table.

"Why do you go only once a month?" Tina asked.

Grandma Mattie turned again looking at her cutting her eyes to the side. The clothes she wore were old, and she wore a grey wig, with Vaseline on her lips to keep them from cracking. She had never remarried again, and she seemed so all alone. She was nearly 70 years old and wore glasses that were wire framed from back in 1919.

"What's wrong with that?" Grandma Mattie asked.

Tina shrugged one thick shoulder, her eyes widening as Grandma Mattie's sharp eyes raked over her.

"Nothing's wrong with it," Tina said.

Grandma Mattie shook her head and cut down on her favorite television show. A sure sign that she was about to go into one of her famous Grandma Mattie rants. "I want you to listen to me and listen good, when you reach my age, and you are on a fixed income, you can only afford to go out once a month, and since my daughter isn't here to help me, I have to watch every penny I get." Plus, and I ain't going to pay no $40.00 for no meal.

Grandma Mattie used to live with her daughter, until a few months ago when suddenly she moved back into her old home after some work had been done on it. From the look of things, it only told me that either she needed more money or the people that did the remodeling didn't know what they were doing. When Tina asked why she left, Grandma Mattie just frowned, crossed her arms and shook her head and said that she and her kids needed their space. Tina frowned because she couldn't understand what that really meant and she didn't bother to question her either.

Tina then replied and said $40.00; Grandma Mattie started to shake her head and laugh.

Grandma Mattie turned again looking at her with her head turned to the side and said, yeah that's right $40.00.

Tina just laughed, and she began to think of how nice it would be if Grandma Mattie could have a nice gentleman friend to take her out every now and then or even come over and watch television to help keep her company.

So Tina decided to suggest this idea to her, she asked her Grandma Mattie; "do you ever think about having a man friend to take you out to the movies or even come and watch television with you?"

Grandma Mattie turned again and said; "How do you know what I need Tina?"

Tina dropped her head and smiled. "I don't know," she said.

Grandma Mattie was from the old school, and she kind of had an idea of what the men were like back in the day. She had been around a whole lot longer than Tina had, and she had covered more grounds than she had. She put her hand on her hip and turned around and said, no Tina, Grandma Mattie don't want as you young folks say "a sugar daddy and I sure don't want a city slicker telling me how much he loves me and asking me if he can rub my back."

Tina looked up with her eyes stretched full of surprise because she couldn't believe that she was hearing her grandma Mattie talking like this. She then said, maybe that's what you need.

Grandma Mattie said quickly again, how do you know what I need Tina?

Tina then began to get a little brave, and she stuck her chest out and said, I don't know what you need Grandma Mattie, It's just that every time that I come over here to visit you. You are sitting in that rocker watching television or reading and rocking back and forth, back and forth.

"Amazed at what Tina had said to her, she replied and said, you know sometimes it just might pay off, me sitting here in this rocking chair rocking all by myself.

Tina couldn't understand why her Grandma Mattie would make such a remark as she did. So she asked her, what do you mean by that Grandma Mattie?

Grandma Mattie was beginning to get beside herself in all the questions that Tina was asking her, so she spoke up and said then I wouldn't have to worry about all the drama these men put you through.

Tina knew her Grandma Mattie very well, and she said I knew that you were going to say that.

Grandma Mattie was on a roll now, so she put her hand on her hip again and said well you know that I'm right.

Tina had begun to realize that she had to think of something quick to say or she wasn't ever going to get Grandma Mattie to agree on letting her fix her up on a blind date. Then she came up with the right thing to say. She said maybe, but Grandma Mattie don't you want a little potion to put some motion in the ocean?

"Looking around and laughing," Grandma Mattie spoke up and said if I want some motion in the ocean, I will go down to the beach and get into the water because I like to go swimming every now and then.

"Now this is what Tina was waiting to hear her granny say, she had finally gotten Grandma Mattie to say something that she would like to do."

Grandma Mattie spoke up and said, now Tina, don't think that you are going to come over here and change me.

Tina jumped right in and said I'm not Grandma Mattie, just listen to me, if you let me fix you up with a blind date and then if you don't like it after you go on it, then you can just shut it down.

Grandma Mattie had begun to look around and think of how lonely it was staying there at the house all by herself since she wasn't living with her daughter and her grandkids anymore. She then said, well I guess it couldn't hurt anything, after all, it does get kind of lonely being here between these four walls.

"There was a sign of relief at that very moment from Tina as she took a deep breath and said, oh Grandma Mattie I'm so glad that you have changed your mind."

"A big smile came across her face, and she said, I don't know about all that, but I guess I can give it a try, but there is just one request that I would like for him to have.

Tina started laughing because she couldn't believe that her granny was making a special request. And what kind of request would this old lady want when she could barely move around. Anyway, Tina said; why sure, Grandma Mattie what is your special request.

Grandma Mattie had started to tell Tina what she wanted when Tina said, wait a minute and let me get some paper and a pen so that I can write your special request down. Because I know how you are when it comes to your special request.

She replied and said "now she couldn't remember what I'm getting ready to tell her. These young folks can't remember anything you say nowadays."

Then Grandma Mattie started telling Tina the things that she has on her list. Now he has to be 6' 2", close to my age, dress with some class, and he's got to have some teeth, I don't want him with just his gums, he has to attend church sometimes, oh and he must have some rhythm, ain't nothing like a man with some rhythm, you know for when you go out dancing.

Tina thought at that very moment, what have I gotten myself into. To look at her, you would think that she was too old to be dancing. So Tina proceeded to ask Grandma Mattie if there were anything else she would like her to add to this list?

Grandma Mattie couldn't think of anything else to add at that moment.

"By the look of the list, Tina knew that she was going to have to go through the loops and hurtles to make sure that she was filling her granny's request."

"Well, with this list, it might take me a little longer, but I'm going to do the very best with your special request," Tina said.

Grandma Mattie replied and said, Good.

"The clock has started to tick, and Tina realizes that she needs to get started on Grandma Mattie's special request." So she tells Grandma Mattie that she is going to be running along and will give her a call a little later.

Meanwhile, Grandma Mattie was thinking if there were anything else that she needed to add to the list that she might have left off. Then she tells Tina if you need anything else, just call me.

Tina then decided that she had better hurry up and leave before Grandma Mattie thinks of something else. She said I'm going to be leaving now Grandma Mattie and I love you.

"I love you too." Grandma Mattie said.

Grandma Mattie started to think about the previous years when she used to go dancing with Pa Paw, so she decided that if she was going to go on a date, she had better get back into the swing of dancing again. So she picks up the phone book and looks up the number of the dance studio. She is so excited now about this idea of having a man in her life again.

"She makes the call to the studio." Hello, yes is this "Shake your Groove Thing Studio?" Oh ok, I wanted to come over there and brush up on my dancing Mm, now I don't want to do the dancing that I've seen some of the girls do on BET. I'm just a little too old to be dropping it like it's hot. Mm yes, tomorrow will be fine. Yes 2:00 is good, ok I'll see you then, thank you.

She sat back down in her rocky chair and started rocking back and forth as usual and thinking about the good time that she might have now since she has decided to go on this date.

CHAPTER TWO

Tina is talking to her girlfriend about GM Mattie's blind date

*I*t's time to come home and relax after church and Tina can't wait to get together with her friend Samantha and share with her the good news about Grandma Mattie. She has finally worn her down in accepting her offer in fixing her up on a blind date. So she invites Samantha to come over after church so that they can have some girl talk.

"Tell me, Tina, how are the plans going with you fixing Grandma Mattie up on a blind date?" Samantha said as she was sitting on the couch relaxed eating a piece of fried chicken and smacking her lip. She had long brownish/black hair with a twist, red lipstick that made her lips look juicy like a red apple, and she dressed like she was a diva at all times.

"Well, I thought that I had already had someone for her till she gave me her list of special request," Tina said.

Samantha looked up with her brown eyes and looked at Tina while she was taking a drink of her peach tea and said, special request, doesn't she realize that her chances of finding a man are slim.

Tina had just fixed a tall glass of peach tea for herself, and she came back into the living room to sit down on the couch.

Well, let's just say that she is depending on me to come through for her.

"Yeah and knowing you as I do, you will," Samantha said.

Tina had gotten really comfortable, and she laid back on the couch with her legs propped up, then she spoke up and said, you know that's right, I really want to see her with someone that she can share her life with, someone that will find her just as exciting as she finds him.

Samantha was still eating on the chicken that she had cooked for them to eat after church, and this was the second piece that she had eaten along with some macaroni and cheese, sweet potatoes, turnip greens, dressed eggs, and hot water cornbread.

Yes, Tina could throw down like that because she had stayed in the kitchen around her mother and Grandma Mattie. "They had shown her how to burn some food as the old folks would say."

"As long as you don't get him off Black People Meet.com, then you should be just fine," Samantha said.

Tina had a secret going on that she hadn't shared with Samantha as of yet, and she wanted to make sure she handled this in a way that she wouldn't be giving herself up. So she spoke up and said, now don't go knocking Black People Meet.com. I've heard some people have met some successful mates off there, besides you can't judge a book by the cover.

What Tina didn't know was that Samantha had other friends that she had been talking to and they had shared some of the things that had gone on, on this site. So she was quick in giving her a reply back.

"You are right, but Betty was telling me that she actually met up with a few of the guys from there. One of them didn't look quite like the picture he had on his site. Plus, he made her pay for their dinner the first night, and the other one failed to mention that he was married with five kids."

Tina looked around with such a funny look on her face and said, well, I know that she sent him sailing.

Samantha loved to gossip you know, so she couldn't wait to finish spilling the tea that Betty had shared with her.

"Actually she didn't, why she had gotten so wrapped up into Jeffrey by the time she thought that she could break it off, it was too late, she had already fallen for him," Samantha said.

Tina had become curious with which one was Jeffrey, so she asked Samantha which one was Jeffrey?

Samantha replied and said, take a wild guess.

Tina got up off the couch with another one of those surprised looks on her face, and her eyes got big, and she said, don't tell me that it was the one that was married.

Yep you are right, and he has been giving her money, taking her shopping, and now I think she has lost her mind. "Why, the next thing you know, he will have her turning flips for chips, you know what I mean."

Why do you say that? Tina said.

Samantha scooted out on the edge of the couch to tell her this, think about it when the Holidays roll around, who do you think he's going to be with? Not her, no, no, no, that's family time.

"This comment had begun to make Tina think about the secret that she had going on. She had begun to get a little nervous, and she was hoping that she wasn't in the same situation."

"I see what you mean," Tina said.

Samantha started laughing and said, you know, just as well as I do that there is no way for her to have a future with this man. He's married and has five kids. He can only be her "Secret Lover.

"Now that you mention it she had better wake up and smell the coffee, or she's going to be left out in the cold," Tina said.

"Samantha started shaking her head and drinking some more peach tea."

Not only left out in the cold, but she might also get hung out to dry. Shoot a lot of those men put that false information down on there and tell you all these nice things, and when they get you right where they want you, then you are the one that winds up getting hurt. Samantha said.

"Sweat had popped out on Tina's face, and she had begun to start getting a little warm. So she picked up one of the church fans that she had laid on the table and started fanning herself with it."

Do you really think that's what they do on there? Tina said.

Samantha got up from the couch and looked over at Tina cause she could see that sweat had popped out on her face and that she was fanning and she said, yes, but wait a minute, are you a member of this site?

"Tina didn't know what to say so she answered saying." Well, what makes you ask me that?

"Why, you sure have been asking a lot of questions." Samantha said

Tina realized that she needed to come clean with her friend and let her in on the secret that she had been keeping from her.

"As a matter of fact I am, and I met this man named Patrick Williams, he seems to be a very nice person," Tina said.

Samantha turned with her mouth open, and she couldn't believe what she had just heard from her friend. She was astonished at what she had just heard.

Girl please now don't you go getting yourself all wrapped up in a "Fatal Attraction." Samantha said.

Tina was thinking more and more on how could she assure her friend and let Samantha know that she got this, and for her not to worry about her.

"Samantha you act like I have the man living here with me," Tina said.

"All I'm saying is just be careful; I would hate to see you get into something that you couldn't get out of that's all," Samantha said.

Tina hurried this conversation along because she could see that her best friend was not very understanding about the decision she has made with this new friend she had.

Thanks, Samantha for the advice, anyway I think that I need to get back to fixing Grandma Mattie up with her blind date. Tina said.

Samantha just shrugged her shoulders and said ok what do you have in mind?

Both of them were really thinking right now who would be best for Tina to fix Grandma Mattie up with. Since Grandma Mattie had given Tina a list of special request.

"I don't really know do you have any suggestions," Tina said.

As Samantha is looking over the list and trying to help her friend find a nice man for Grandma Mattie, she suddenly remembers that this description covers the security guard that worked at her bank.

"Wait a minute I think that I know just who you could fix her up with, and I think that she is going to like him," Samantha said.

Tina looked over at her with an amazing look on her face and said who?

Mr. Berry Washington, he is a security guard that works at the bank where Samantha has an account. He is about 6' 2," and he is so nice, looks good and she has noticed his finger before, he doesn't wear a wedding ring, and when she walks by him, he always smells good.

"His name is Mr. Berry Washington; you know that man that works part-time at the bank as a security guard," Samantha said.

Tina starts smiling and laughing with joy hoping that this will be a good man for her granny. She looks over at Tina and says, why didn't I think about him, he is tall, looks good, and he's very nice and polite.

Yes, he is, and I think that they would make a nice couple, as long as he doesn't say something like. "I got broads in Atlanta," Samantha said.

Knowing Grandma Mattie like Tina does, she knows what her granny would say if he said something like that to her, because she does not play. She pictured her in her mind standing there with her hand on her hip.

Well knowing my Grandma Mattie she would say, "and I won't be your side chic in Atlanta."

Samantha starts laughing, and she came back with the reply, I know that's right.

"All I need to do now is a background check on him, and it will be done," Tina said.

Meanwhile, Samantha had some thoughts of some things that would help make the date run smooth. She said, just make sure that he has plenty of cash for the big bash and a reliable ride.

"Oh, I wouldn't have it any other way for my Grandma Mattie," Tina said.

Samantha gets up and goes to get her another piece of chicken, a glass of peach tea, as well as a piece of chest cake and comes back into the living room, feeling happy for the results that she had helped her best friend Tina come up with for Grandma Mattie.

"I just can't believe it, Grandma Mattie is trying to get her groove back like Stella got her groove back," Samantha said.

Tina said, stop that; she deserves to have somebody in her life to make her happy.

Samantha started to laugh and rock back and forth on the couch. She bursts out with, oh! He's going to make her happy alright. Why, he will have her feeling like that song "I'm so into you, and I don't know what I'm going to do.

They both started laughing and drinking their peach tea and eating their chest cake, and they said, everything is set now, all we have to do is wait and see what happens. Afterward, Samantha got Mr. Washington's number for Tina to call him.

CHAPTER THREE

GM Mattie Is At Home Thinking About Her Blind Date & Paw Pa

Grandma Mattie is at home sitting in her rocky chair watching her favorite television show rocking back and forth, back & forth. When all of a sudden her phones rings, and she picks it up and answers it, only to find out that it's her granddaughter Tina.

Hello, she said.

Tina is on the other end of the line laughing and full of excitement because she can't wait to tell her granny that she has fixed her up on a blind date and she is going to take her shopping.

"Hello Grandma Mattie, I just wanted to tell you that I finally have your blind date for you and I think that you are going to like him," Tina said.

"As Tina starts telling Grandma Mattie about her blind date, she starts to have a great big grin come across her face." It was really beginning to sink in with her now that this wasn't a dream. She was really going on a blind date with someone tall and handsome that could rock her world beyond what she could imagine, in a good way of course.

"Is that so," Grandma Mattie said.

Yes, and I wanted to tell you that I'm going to take you shopping for something new for your date. So what would be a good day for you to go before Saturday?

"Grandma Mattie gets to thinking about all the things that she has to do before that day."

Well I have Bible study on Wednesday, Thursday I have my dance class, so I guess that it will have to be on Friday at noon. Just as long as I get back in time to see my favorite television show. Grandma Mattie said.

Tina had a thought on what Grandma Mattie had just said to her, and she was really happy that her granny was getting ready for that big day that Tina was planning for her. This was all Tina had wanted, to see her granny get out of that rocky chair and start living life again.

"Did I hear you say that you have a dance class on Thursday?" Tina said.

Grandma Mattie smiled and said, that's right.

"Well, how long have you been taking these dance classes, Grandma Mattie?" Tina said.

Grandma Mattie started laughing and said oh I've been taking them for about a week and a half now.

Tina started imagining how Grandma Mattie would look on that day in her new outfit and how she would be dancing with Mr. Washington on that day. This was the happiness that Tina had intended for her granny to have. Tina was so happy for her granny; she couldn't wait to take her shopping.

"I see," said Tina.

You see Grandma Mattie, and Paw Pa used to go dancing a lot when he was alive. They had been engaged in a few dancing contests over the years and won a few as well. So it wasn't anything new to her. And once she took the class, it all started coming back to her. Now don't get it twisted she could dance. He better hope that he can keep up with her.

"You see, Grandma Mattie had to brush up on her dancing skills cause it's been a while since I've been out dancing." Grandma Mattie said.

Tina realized at that very moment that Grandma Mattie got some skills and she wasn't afraid to use them. And maybe she could teach me a few things.

"Well, there is nothing wrong with that GM Mattie, in fact, you beat me to the punch," Tina said.

Grandma Mattie started laughing and said, I'm sorry Tina.

It crossed Tina's mind while she was talking to her granny, where she had inherited some of her wisdom and knowledge from. She had a strong mind and soul like her Grandma, even though she wasn't as old as she was. She could still feel and see the resemblance that they shared, and it was great to know that she could still share and see this with her.

"Oh there is no need to be sorry Grandma Mattie, I'm just glad that you are working out now," Tina said.

Grandma Mattie was older, and she always wanted to be on time, so she asked Tina what time should she be ready.

"We can leave at about 1:00 in the evening on Friday, if that's alright with you," Tina said.

"That will be fine Tina, so I will see you then," Grandma Mattie said.

They both said their goodbyes and got off the phone.

Grandma Mattie then walks over to the table and picks up her and Paw Pa family picture, and as she looked at it, tears began to form in her eyes. Then as she was gazing at their photo, she began to talk to the picture.

Well, Paw Pa, I just want to tell you that I will always love you and I will never forget all the good times that we used to have, and I still miss you singing to me at night. It's been a long time since I've been excited about going somewhere. I hope that you understand Paw Pa. Tina has fixed me up on this blind date for Saturday, so I just wanted you to know what I was going to do, and I hope that it's alright with you. Oh, and I've been taking some dance classes to brush up on my dancing skills, why I used to remember when we would go dancing, and we would have the best time. I really do miss you, but I know that we will be together one day. Until then I think that I will try to see if I can pass some time away with this new blind date. That is if he's any good, of course, you know that I'm going to be on my best behavior. "Laughing" hugs and kisses Paw Pa.

Grandma Mattie puts the photo down and picks up her Bible and starts reading sitting there in her rocking chair.

CHAPTER FOUR

Tina Takes Grandma Mattie Shopping for her date

Tina and Grandma Mattie have arrived at the store where she's going to find her something for her big night out in town. Tina said, let's go in here, and then they walked in and started to look around when one of the sales clerks came over to assist them.

"Hello Ladies, how can I help you? " Barbara said.

"Yes, I'm looking for something special for my Grandma Mattie. You see she has a date soon and she is a little old fashion, and I wanted something that will make her feel good about herself and look good on her." Tina said.

The store clerk is a middle age lady with some specs of gray in her hair, she wears glasses, and she knows how to wear her makeup and how to dress.

Well, come right this way I have a special rack just for her. Barbara said.

"So they all walk over to the sale rack and start looking through the different outfits that they have on sale.

"Here they are, and you can try on as many of them as you like," Barbara said.

Tina and Grandma Mattie continue to look, and Tina finds three different outfits that she really likes and she tells her to take the dresses to the dressing room and try them on. Grandma Mattie agreed.

"The dressing room is right over here," Barbara said.

Grandma Mattie is in the dressing room trying on the dresses when she gets to thinking about how she felt in her younger days when she was getting ready to go out to the town. She felt full of life and some inspiration once again. She comes out after she tries the first one on.

"Oh, Grandma Mattie, that really looks nice on you, how do you like it?" Tina said.

Grandma Mattie replied well it looks alright.

Tina looked at her and said you don't have to choose that one you have a few more to try on that you can choose from.

When Grandma Mattie came out of the dressing room this time, she was feeling this dress, she came out twisting and prancing around. Tina can really tell that she likes this one better than she did the other one.

Aw sucky, sucky now, I can't tell you nothing. Well, he's going to be saying "there goes my baby," Tina said.

"Do you really think so?" Grandma Mattie said.

Tina looked at her granny and she could see the glow in her eyes and the smile on her face. She said, why not you are beautiful, and you got some swag about yourself, Grandma Mattie.

Grandma Mattie turned and looked at Tina with a look that will kill and said, what do you mean by "I have swag?"

"Laughing and moving back and forth clutching her purse Tina said, well, it's a term that the young folks use nowadays, when you know how to dress and how to carry yourself. In other words, you have it going on. Tina said.

Grandma Mattie said oh ok, telling me I got swag I didn't know why you were calling me, then she said I want this one, I really like this one.

"Then we will get this one for you and get you some accessories and a nice pair of shoes," Tina said.

While Tina was at the counter paying for everything, Grandma Mattie sees a purse that she likes. She picks it up and tells Tina, oh you can pay for this too. Then she heads for the door and says I will meet you in the car. Tina shook her head and asked the clerk how much was that purse she took. The clerk told her how much the purse was and Tina swallowed and said I wasn't expecting that.

CHAPTER FIVE
Today is the day for Grandma Mattie to meet her man

Well, this is the big day for Grandma Mattie to meet her man. She has gotten ready and she looks good. She has a long black flowered dress on with her pearl earrings and necklace, black shoes and her face looks really nice with the makeup that Tina has helped her with. Even the red lipstick that she picked out makes her look younger than she was before she had this makeover done.

"Are you excited about tonight?" Tina said.

"Grandma Mattie replied and said, Tina, this is all I've been thinking about since you had asked me to go on this date."

Tina then thought about how her granny story could relate to one of the characters that she used to watch on television when she was a little girl.

"Just think of it as if you were Cinderella going to the ball," Tina said.

Grandma Mattie replied and said, "if you say so."

Tina looked at her, and she could see again how happy she had made her Grandma Mattie feel. This is something that she hadn't seen in her for a very long time. Her smile stretched across her face, and she was glowing like a lit up Christmas tree. Not to mention that she looked twenty years younger.

"I do, I just want you to have a good time and live a little," Tina said.

Grandma Mattie said well, I'm doing this for you because you were so thrilled on getting me hooked up with someone.

"At this particular time, Tina couldn't hold her composure, she started laughing, and she said, oh Grandma Mattie, you are going to be just fine, and you can thank me later."

Grandma Mattie suddenly had a moment of doubt going through her mind, and she felt like she needed to ask Tina about the list that she had given her.

"I would like to ask you something though Tina." Grandma Mattie said.

Tina replied and said, what is it, Grandma Mattie?

Grandma Mattie turned and looked at Tina with one of those looks, and she was serious too. Now did you make sure he had all the things that I had down on the list that I gave you?

Tina could see that Grandma Mattie was serious and she had better answer here in the right way or there might not be a night out in town.

"Let's just say that I tried to go by the list that you gave me and I might have missed a few things, but this is the closest that I could get to what you wanted," Tina said.

Grandma Mattie looked around at Tina again and said just tell me one thing, is he 6ft 2in?

Then Tina looked at Grandma Mattie and started wondering, why was it so important for this man to be 6' 2" tall, she wanted to ask her, but she was scared to, but she knew if she ever wanted to find out the reason, now would be a good time to ask her. "Laughing" she said yes he is, tell me why he has to be that tall.

"The doorbell rings and Grandma Mattie was thinking of how she got out of telling her that story right now." Well just get the door, and I will have to tell you about it a little later.

Tina replied and said alright and then she goes over to the door to let Mr. Washington in.

When Tina opens the door, she sees Mr. Washington standing there in his black suit, smelling good with a smile on his face. She could tell that he was just as excited for this date as her granny was.

She then said come on in and come right this way. I would like for you to meet my Grandma Mattie.

"Good Evening Ms. Mattie pleased to meet you, and these flowers are for you." Mr. Washington said.

Grandma Mattie was standing there smiling, and she said, thank you for the flowers.

Mr. Washington replied and said, you are very welcome.

Tina felt like now would be a good time for her to leave the room and let them get acquainted, so she said I'm going into the other room and if you need me just call me.

"Finally after standing there looking him up and down and smiling, she asked him would you like to have a seat?" Grandma Mattie said. And she replied to Tina and said ok.

Mr. Washington was standing there starring back with a great big grin on his face too, and he replied and said, yes I would, thank you.

When they both had sat down, Grandma Mattie put the flowers in her vase. She asked him if he would like to have something to drink.

"No thank you but thanks for asking me. I wanted to let you know that I have made all the plans for this evening, unless it's somewhere else special that you would like to go." Mr. Washington said.

Grandma Mattie started thinking about how Mr. Washington was a man that likes to take charge and make the plans. I already like him she said to herself. Then she spoke up and said, no, I'm sure what you have planned for us will do just fine.

Alright then, Tina has told me so much about you.

"During this time Grandma Mattie was just smiling and sitting there looking him up and down, and suddenly she says, she has, well, I wish that I could say the same."

Mr. Washington replied and said, excuse me.

Grandma Mattie immediately realized that she might have said something negative, so she had better find the right words to straighten up what she had said. She then said, what I meant to say was she wanted you to be a surprise for me, and boy you are a surprise alright.

Mr. Washington still smiling reared back in his seat and said, is that good or bad.

"It is good, what I meant to say is that she has good taste like her Grandma Mattie that's all." Grandma Mattie said.

"That's nice. Well, I guess we had better get going. I have our reservation made for 7:00 p.m." Mr. Washington said.

Grandma Mattie stood up and calls Tina into the room and then she says, ok I just need to get my purse, and I will be right back, Tina can you help me?

"Tina replied and said sure, excuse us, Mr. Washington."

Grandma Mattie goes into the bedroom to get her purse and Tina goes into the bedroom with her. Then Tina asked her, well what do you think about him? Grandma Mattie grabs her hand and says, baby he is fine as wine, and I just want to say thank you from the bottom of my heart, thank you, thank you, thank you.

Meanwhile, Mr. Washington overheard them talking, and his smile got bigger than it was before and he straightened his necktie up and ran his hand over his hair, and he knew that this was going to be a night to remember.

"You are welcome Grandma Mattie; now I will wait up for you to get back if you want me to," Tina said.

Grandma Mattie grabbed her purse turned back around and looked at her and said, there is no need for you to do that, your Grandma Mattie got this, she got it.

Tina looked back at her with a surprised look and said, are you sure you don't want me to? I "don't mind staying here till you get back.

No, you can go on home I got it from here just make sure that you lock up before you leave." Grandma Mattie said.

Tina really wasn't worried about her granny being out with Mr. Washington. She just wanted to be there for her when she got back home. But Tina could see that her granny didn't want her treating her like she was a teenager. So she said well if you say so, but if you need me for anything just call me ok.

"Ok, but I don't think that I'm going to need you for anything. Not a thing you hear me?" Grandma Mattie said.

Tina replied and said ok Grandma Mattie, well, I hope that you have a good time.

Grandma Mattie kept looking into the living room at Mr. Washington and looking back at Tina laughing, and she then said, don't worry Grandma Mattie is planning on it.

Then they went to the living room where Mr. Washington was waiting and Grandma Mattie looked over to Mr. Washington and said, "I'm ready."

Mr. Washington stands up and says alright, he begins to thank Tina for fixing him and Ms. Mattie up on this date. Then he turns and looks at Ms. Mattie and says ladies first and let me get the door for you. Again he thanked Tina for arranging the date, and he said I really do appreciate it.

Tina replied, you are most certainly welcome, "Shaking his hand."

As they are walking out the door, Tina says you all have a good time now. Then she gets her purse and locks up and goes home.

CHAPTER SIX

They arrive at the restaurant and wait to be seated

They have arrived at the restaurant to be seated as the host Sandra greets them as they walk in. She is a very nice young lady, and she already has their table ready for them, and she says, "Welcome to Shell Moore's Restaurant," do you have a reservation for this evening?

"Yes we do, the name is Mr. Barry Washington," Mr. Washington said,

Sandra looked down at the registry to find their reservation, and then she said oh yes, Mr. Washington there you are and your table is ready, right this way, please. She shows them their table.

Mr. Washington then pulls the chair out for Ms. Mattie while she had a sit. Ms. Mattie says to herself, well he's alright. She realizes that she has been missing this kind of treatment. This was better than watching Gun Smoke right now. Still smiling she did feel like she was Cinderella.

Sandra then gives them their menu after they were seated, then she said, the waitress will be with you momentarily, enjoy. They said thank you, she replied and said you are very welcome and then she walks away.

While they were silently seated, looking over their menus, Mr.

Washington looks up and looks over to Ms. Mattie and says, well how do you like the restaurant, Ms. Mattie?

"It's a very nice place, and I wanted to thank you for agreeing to meet with me and take me on this date." Ms. Mattie said.

Mr. Washington looked up and smiled at her and said it is my pleasure Ms. Mattie. So can you tell me something about yourself so that I can get to know you a little better?

Grandma Mattie laid the menu down and said well, I don't know where to start.

"Just take your time, I'm not in a hurry, and I want you to feel comfortable." Mr. Washington said.

Grandma Mattie was feeling a little nervous, but she knew she had to keep the conversation going because she really liked this so well, she wanted to go out again with this man. So she spoke up and said, well as you know I live by myself, I go out once a month with some of the ladies from the church. I like going to the plays, picnics, and the movies every now and then.

Well, what a coincident, I like going to some of the same places, and I hang out with the deacons from the church. Mr. Washington said.

Ms. Mattie replied, oh really.

"At this moment the waiter came over and introduced herself as Rochelle, she seemed nice, and she was cute too. She said I will be your waiter for this evening, have you had a chance to look at the menu? If you are ready, I will take your order now."

Mr. Washington looks over at Ms. Mattie and says are you ready to order now?

"Yes, I believe that I will have the special for this evening." Ms. Mattie said.

Then Mr. Washington looks up to the waiter Rochelle and says, we will have two specials for the evening. Then he looks back over to Ms. Mattie and says, would you like to have some wine to drink with your meal or would you like to have something of your choice?

"Wine is fine," Ms. Mattie said.

Mr. Washington then proceeds to tell the waiter to bring them their best bottle of wine. She said "Yes Sir, and will that be all.

"Yes at the moment, thank you, now where were we?" Mr. Washington said.

Ms. Mattie looked up at him sitting across the table smiling and says, well I was just about to ask you to tell me something about you.

Soft music starts to play.

Mr. Washington clears his throat and says do you mind if I tell you after this song is over.

Ms. Mattie replied and said, why not at all.

Mr. Washington took a long look at Ms. Mattie and said would you give me the honor of dancing with me Ms. Mattie.

Ms. Mattie's mind started working overtime as she said to herself well I guess this is going to be interesting, I haven't been held this close in a long time. My fluffy pillow is the closest thing that I've held in a very long time. Then she spoke up and said, why, sure I would love to.

They get up and proceed to the floor to dance, and afterward, he walks her back to the table.

Mr. Washington walks her back over to the table and pulls out her chair for her. And after he takes his seat he tells her, thank you, Ms. Mattie, for the dance.

"Thank you for asking me." Ms. Mattie said.

The waiter came back to the table with their wine and dinner. She pours the wine and says, is there anything else that I can get for you. They said no. She said, well enjoy, and I will check back with you in a few minutes.

"They both replied and said alright."

Mr. Washington looked over across the table looking at Ms. Mattie and folded his hand around his wine glass and picked it up and said, let's have a toast. Let's toast to you Ms. Mattie, to a beautiful lady with a very nice smile, not to mention that you look gorgeous in that dress that you are wearing and I would love to take you out again if you would let me.

Ms. Mattie folded her hand around her glass and smiled at Mr. Washington and said, I would love to do that. And thank you for the compliment.

"You are quite welcome, Ms. Mattie." Mr. Washington said.

They had been eating for a few minutes when all of a sudden Mr. Washington looked over to Ms. Mattie and said how do you like your dinner, Ms. Mattie?

Ms. Mattie replied and said it is really good, thank you for asking.

Mr. Washington looked over across the table and said, good, because if you didn't like it, I was going to let you order something else.

Ms. Mattie looked up at Mr. Washington and said thank you, but it's just fine. She was beginning to think that she was in the "Twilight Zone" she started looking around for the candid camera that they always come out with when they are playing a joke on you.

I must say that I've really enjoyed this evening and this beautiful lady that I'm with. How about you? Mr. Washington said.

Ms. Mattie replied and said it's been a wonderful evening, I'm really glad that I came.

Good Mr. Washington said. He cleared his throat again and looked over to her again and said can I ask you something Ms. Mattie?

Why sure Ms. Mattie replied?

Mr. Washington reached across the table and grabbed her hand and looked into her eyes and said would you like to go out with me again at your convenience.

Ms. Mattie was beginning to blush at this very moment, and she felt like a little girl all shy and giggly. Then she said I would love to on one condition.

"Yes, I'm listening." Mr. Washington said.

Ms. Mattie was hoping that she wouldn't get her face broke as the young folks say. So she took a deep breath and said I would like for you to attend church with me sometimes.

Mr. Washington smiled and looked at Ms. Mattie looking straight into her eyes and said I can do that and sometimes we can attend my church as well.

"Laughing" that is a deal then. Ms. Mattie said.

They have finished eating, and the waiter comes back over to the table to see how their dinner was. Then she asked them if they were interested in having some dessert. She poured some more wine and then she removed the dishes right after they said that they would not be having dessert.

"Ms. Mattie thanked Mr. Washington again for such a lovely evening and then she told him how delicious the meal was."

They laughed and talked for a while and then he asked her if she was ready to go and they left.

CHAPTER SEVEN

The next day Tina meets with GM Mattie to see how her date went

It's the next day, and Grandma Mattie is sitting up in the living room thinking about what a good time she had last night with Mr. Washington, looking every now and then at her and Paw, Pa's picture. She loved Paw, Pa and she will never forget him. But last night was something special that she could have if she would just let go and let God work a miracle. She hears the knock at the door and says come in.

"Tina walks through the door smiling, looking over at Grandma Mattie, and she said good morning, well you know why I'm over here, you have got to tell me all the juicy details about your date that you had last night."

Grandma Mattie started smiling and looked over at me when suddenly I notice she was still wearing the make-up that I had put on her face from the night before. She had also added some fresh lipstick.

Well, it was really nice I must say that it brought back a lot of old memories of when your Paw, Pa was living, anyway the first thing we did was go to this really nice restaurant, and we had dinner and danced while we were there. Then we came home and looked up at the stars for a while and then he walked me to the door, and we said our good-byes, and he left.

"Tina smiled and said aw that was really nice." Did you kiss him?

She started shaking her head back and forth and turned to Tina and said, why, no I didn't kiss him.

Tina couldn't understand why she didn't kiss him and why she was so quick to answer her when all of a sudden Grandma Mattie jumped up out of the chair and headed over to the couch where Tina was sitting. Tina just knew that she was about to chew her out for what she said. Then she pointed her finger at me and said, let me tell you a little secret Tina. You never kiss a man on your first date.

"Another surprising look came over Tina's face, and she said and why not Grandma Mattie?"

"Because if you don't kiss him then. He will be curious until he meets you again to try to get one. And that's what makes it special." Grandma Mattie said.

Tina replied and said oh ok, I see now what you mean Grandma Mattie.

"Look, Tina, you have to see where a man is coming from before you put all your eggs in one basket. You hear me." Grandma Mattie said.

Tina dropped her head and then she turned and looked up at Grandma Mattie with her innocent eyes and said what do you mean?

Well, when I was a young lady coming up, you dated them more than one or two nights before you got serious with each other and then he had to speak of marriage. Cause nowadays; I know that it's a whole lot different. You ladies nowadays think that you have to do everything on your first date. I want you to listen and listen clearly to me, a real man that really likes you and is willing to wait, he will be there for you, and that's the truth.

"I've been waiting for the right man Grandma Mattie, but I feel like I'm running out of time," Tina said.

The spirit of the Lord came over Grandma Mattie she wanted to make sure that she was telling her granddaughter the right things. The right things that would help her as she begun to go out into the world, she said let me ask you something Tina have you been praying?

"Yes, but I feel like sometimes God does not hear my prayers," Tina said.

Grandma Mattie smiled and grabbed her hand and said, Tina, he hears you, and he will come in his time, not yours. That's what wrong with a lot of us folks today. We get in a big hurry of wanting him to answer right away. Have you ever thought that you might not be ready yet to handle a relationship?

Tina thought for a few minutes and then she looked up and said, now that you put it like that, I am kind of busy right now trying to go back to school, and I'm still living off the trust funds that mom and dad gave me.

"You see God knows what's best for us when we think otherwise." Grandma Mattie said.

"I see what you mean Tina replied."

Now that Grandma Mattie had explained some things to Tina, she felt like she had given her the lesson that she needs while she is waiting for her man.

"So just give it some time, and one day you will look up, and it will happen." Grandma Mattie said.

Tina always had looked up to her granny, and she had always listened to her advice. That day she took those words of wisdom to heart and realized that what her Grandma was telling her was right.

"Alright Grandma Mattie I hear you, and I will continue to pray. Now when is your next date with Mr. Washington?" Tina said.

"He has left the next one up to me. So I asked him to go to church with me sometimes." Grandma Mattie said.

That's nice, Tina replied.

Grandma Mattie jumped up off the couch clapping her hand and walking around and then she took a seat in her rocking chair. She looked over to Tina and said. Oh and since the 4th of July Holiday is just around the corner. I was thinking about having a backyard party and inviting the family over to see how things go with Mr. Washington meeting the family.

Well just leave it up to me, and I will make it happen. Just let me know what you want to have, and I will get started on it for you. Tina said.

While they were talking and exchanging ideas about the food that they were going to have at the party, Tina notices again how happy she has made her granny. She knows now that she has done a good thing for her, and she won't ever forget it.

CHAPTER EIGHT

Grandma Mattie is having a Backyard Party

This is the day of the backyard party, and Tina has invited a lot of family and friends. Oh and Uncle Jessie is there. That's one of Grandma Mattie's sons; you see he has a little problem sometimes with his liquid, but he is still family. It's almost time for Grandma Mattie and Mr. Washington to arrive, so let's see what's going on with the party while everyone is waiting.

"Now Uncle Jessie, you can't be putting any liquid in the punch, because it's not that kind of party," Tina said.

It's not replied Uncle Jessie.

"No it's not," Tina said.

Uncle Jessie was in his late fifties, and he wore a beard. He was tall nice looking and dressed fairly well. Seeing him like this was a whole lot different from what he used to be. You know Uncle Jessie hadn't always been like this, but over time, life weighs down on some people to where they change a little. He said and why not?

"Looking over at Uncle Jessie, she then said because this is the day that the rest of the family gets to meet Grandma Mattie's man friend," Tina said.

Uncle Jessie replied and said mom got a man.

Tina started laughing and looked at Uncle Jessie and said, yes she got a man, and I want you to be on your best behavior.

Uncle Jessie seemed confused there for a moment, and he scratched his head and kept saying, Mom's got a man; Mom's got a man. Then he walked away.

Mom Margie was one of Grandma Mattie's daughters, she was tall with a cute cut hairstyle, dangling earrings, and she knew how to dress too. She was married to daddy Bob.

"How is everything going Tina?" Margie said.

Tina turned to mom Margie and said everything would be fine as long as I can keep Uncle Jessie out of the punch. You know how he likes to turn up, all I need is to have everybody walking around her with a buzz.

Mom Margie replied and said, and if that happens, your Grandma Mattie will be fit to be tied.

"Believe me I know," Tina said.

Daddy Bob was walking around helping Tina make sure everything was going alright with the family and guest. He was a very nice son-in-law that had always helped the family out financially. He was medium height, clean cut and always wore his hats.

"Tina, your grandma Mattie should be here pretty soon. Is everything ready?" Daddy Bob said.

Tina said yes dad, as long as I can keep Uncle Jessie out of the punch. Can you do me a favor dad and keep your eye on him for me.

Sure, Tina, Daddy Bob said.

Tina shook her head and hugged him and said thank you, that's one less thing that I will have to worry about.

The party is jumping now, the guys have started playing cards, and the music is going, and it looks like everyone is having a good time.

Tina walked over to Bennie and asked: "how is the meat coming along Bennie?"

Bennie was a good friend of the family, he was tall, handsome and he was always smart in school. He was always on the honor roll, and he was a lady man too. Yeah, he never wanted for anything.

"We should be ready to eat soon," Bennie said.

Tina smiled at him and said, I just want to make sure that we have everything ready for when Grandma Mattie gets here.

"Bennie replied and said." Leave it up to me. I haven't let you down yet, have I?

"No Bennie that is the reason I always ask you to grill for me for all of our cook-outs, because I can always count on you," Tina said.

Bennie turned the meat over and took some water and poured over the fire and looked over to Tina and said. I know that's right.

"Hey everyone get ready, here comes Grandma Mattie and her friend." Mom Margie said.

Grandma Mattie & Mr. Washington walks into the Backyard party to join the family. Then Tina walks over and says Hello Mr. Washington good to see you again and shakes his hand and then she hugs Grandma Mattie. "Welcome to our family Backyard party," Tina said.

"Why thank you, Tina, Mr. Washington said."

Grandma Mattie starts looking around to see all who were there. Then she said, I see almost everybody was able to make it.

"Yes, and I hope that you all are going to have a good time," Tina said.

Mr. Washington spoke up and said I'm sure we will.

Grandma Mattie was grinning from ear to ear, and she wore her favorite red knee knockers, white blouse, red checked vest, and her cotton socks with her dingy looking shoes.

"Well let me introduce you to the rest of my family and friends." Grandma Mattie said.

Grandma Mattie goes around and starts introducing Mr. Washington to most of the family when Uncle Jessie goes over and looks at the punch. Daddy Bob looks at him and shakes his head. Uncle Jessie looks back and shakes his head and walks away. As he is walking away, he walks over to Grandma Mattie and Mr. Washington. She says this is my son Jessie, Uncle Jessie offers Mr. Washington a drink, and he says, no thank you. Grandma Mattie says Jessie go on; nobody wants to drink that mess but you.

More of the music starts playing, and Mr. Washington asks Ms. Mattie if she would like to have a seat. They took a seat, and Tina walks over and brings both of them a glass of punch. They said thank you. Mr. Washington then said, so this is your family?

"Most of them are and a few of my friends but this isn't all of them." Grandma Mattie said.

Mr. Washington was looking around and seeing all of her family and friends. Seeing how nice it was to see that they cared enough for her to gather like this. And he said it seems like you have a lovely family and friends.

"Why thank you," Grandma Mattie said.

Meanwhile, Tina looked over at Grandma Mattie and Mr. Washington and said do you think that they are enjoying themselves?

"Mom Margie said, yes, I believe they are, looking at them. And he's not bad looking."

Tina smiled and said you are right about that; Grandma Mattie said that I had good taste like her. Tina then says excuse me I'm going to have to cut Uncle Jessie off from going to that punch bowl again.

Bennie shouts out you know what time it is. The music starts playing Backyard Party, and most of them get up and do the electric slide line dance. This is always a family tradition. Everybody is laughing and having a good time.

"Would you like something to eat." Grandma Mattie said.

Mr. Washington rubbed his stomach and looked over to Ms. Mattie and said I'm still full from the popcorn that we had at the movie. I will just take a plate home if you don't mind.

Grandma Mattie replied and said that's quite alright with me. Then she motions for Tina to come over to where they were sitting. Tina comes over and says, yes what do you need Grandma Mattie. She said can you fix Mr. Washington and I a plate to take with us. She replied and said ok.

"Grandma Mattie looked over at Mr. Washington and said, I'm glad that you enjoyed yourself."

Mr. Washington turned and looked at her and said with a smile on his face, yes I did, there is nothing like having family around. You see this reminds me of some of the family gatherings that my family have each year.

Grandma Mattie replied and said, you are right there is nothing like family. Then she said well, it is getting late and I guess we had better be going.

"Mr. Washington said alright, and then he stood up and started waving and saying goodbye to everyone."

Tina then started walking over to Mr. Washington and Grandma Mattie and handed them their plate and said, I hope that you all enjoyed yourself and I hope that you come back again, Mr. Washington.

They both replied and said that they did and then everyone shouted bye and waved bye to them, and they left.

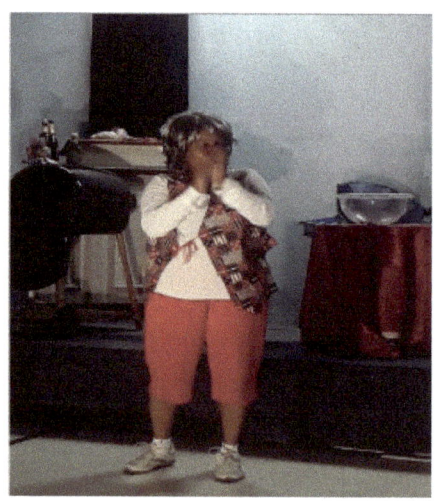

CHAPTER NINE

Grandma Mattie talks to Tina on what a good time she had

It's Sunday morning, and Tina is up earlier than usual because she wanted to go over and visit her Grandma Mattie before church starts. The doorbell rings and Grandma Mattie says come in. Tina walks in smiling and goes over and hugs her granny and kisses her.

Well, what brings you over this early in the morning? Grandma Mattie said.

Tina gets all comfortable on the couch and turns to look at her granny and says, I just had to come over before going to church, and find out how you and Mr. Washington liked the Backyard Party that we had yesterday?

Grandma Mattie turned smiling again and said he loved it, and I did too. In fact, he liked the party and my family so well. He wants us all to attend church with him in October for the Pastor Anniversary.

"Oh really now," Tina replied.

Yes, he does, and I told him that we would be there and that I'm really looking forward to having worship services with him. I just hope that everyone will be on their best behavior again, especially my son Jessie. Grandma Mattie said.

Tina looked at Grandma Mattie, and she could see that she was worried about Uncle Jessie attending the church drunk. So she reassured her and said don't worry yourself about that, I will make sure that Uncle Jessie is ready and that he will be on his best behavior.

"Ok, Tina and I wanted to thank you again for setting me up with Mr. Washington and for helping me with the Back Yard Party. Everything was really nice, and I won't ever forget it." Grandma Mattie said.

Tina could see a tear come into her granny's eye. She walked over and hugged her and said, it was my pleasure Grandma Mattie, I just wanted to do something special for you, since you are always doing special things for the family and me.

And baby you did, you have made Grandma Mattie so happy. Well, I haven't been this happy since Paw, Pa was living. I feel like I've been given another chance in life. Well, that man got Grandma Mattie feeling pretty good right now, yes he does.

Tina said well, I'm just glad that you are happy. Now I've just got to ask you this one question, Grandma Mattie.

"What is it, Tina?" Grandma Mattie said.

Tina sat back over on the crouch out of reaching distance, just in case Grandma Mattie was going to reach for her. Then she asked her did you kiss him this time.

Grandma Mattie laughed and looked at Tina and said, Tina, Grandma Mattie can't lie, he tore my lips up, and I tore his up too. Yes, I did, and I'm glad that I still knew how to do it. It was like Campbell soup, Mmm Good.

Tina laughed and said "well Grandma Mattie I'm so glad that you finally got to kiss him this time."

"Yes, and I am too because I had been dreaming of how it would be when he kissed me. And it was just like I saw it and felt it in my dream." Grandma Mattie said.

Tina started thinking of how it would be someday for her. She was hoping that it would be just as amazing as it was for her granny. Then she said maybe one day I will get to have that feeling with that special someone.

"Grandma Mattie looked over at Tina and said you will Tina, just remember what I said."

Tina replied and said I will, Grandma Mattie.

GRANDMA MATTIE GETS HER MAN

Grandma Mattie had a puzzled look on her face and was staring out into space. Then Tina spoke and said, what is it Grandma Mattie, is there something wrong?

"He seems like he's a good man and he knows how to treat a lady. But I'm getting some kind of spirit from him, Tina." Grandma Mattie said.

"Tina replied and said is it a good spirit or a bad one she asked."

No, now it's a good one, I just can't seem to figure him out. I feel like he's a God fearing man with good potential. So I'm just going to continue to pray a little more on this and ask God to show me more about him.

"And he will Grandma Mattie; he will show up and show out right on time. At least that's what you have always told us". Tina said.

"Grandma Mattie replied and said, yes I have, haven't I?"

Tina then grabbed her hand and said besides you've got to give it some time. You all have only been dating for a little while.

"Yeah, I guess you can say that I'm a little anxious about this, because this is something that is new to me, and when you've been with someone as long as I was with Paw Pa, you can't think of anything else but him." Grandma Mattie said,

Tina hugs her again and says Grandma Mattie I know that you miss him and things will never be the same, but you can give yourself a chance to be happy again. By going out and by doing some of the things that you used to do.

"Why sure I can, and that's just what I'm going to do, well I guess that I had better start getting ready for church." Grandma Mattie said. Tina hugged her and said I will see you in church then. Bye.

AFTERWORD

This story is based on a grandmother who lost her husband some years ago. She has been living by Herself, and she attends church and outings with some of the ladies from the church. One day her granddaughter Tina decides that she wanted to find a gentleman friend for her grandmother because she was tired of seeing her alone. She gets together with her girlfriend, and they thought of introducing her to Mr. Washington, the security guard. This is how Grandma Mattie got her man. Betty Britton is playing the role of Grandma Mattie; she is a Writer, Producer, Director, Actor, Sign Language (Beginner -ASL), Computer Oriented of her own production company. She also does Photography and Wedding planning. Betty has also been on television in "Noah Knows Best, HBO Comedy Special w/Jeff Foxworthy & Bill Engvall and Channel Five New Documentary."

AFTERWORD

www.ingramcontent.com/pod-product-compliance
Lightning Source LLC
Chambersburg PA
CBHW062029290426
44108CB00025B/2831